The Dating D⚲ck

A Journey of the Heart

By Dee Aspin

The Dating Dock, A Journey of the Heart

Scriptural References

Disclaimer: These stories are based on actual incidences. They may sound like someone you know who has similar situations. Confidentiality has been observed in certain cases and names or minor circumstances have been changed.

Bibliography of other references are in the back of the book.

Special thanks:

- 🛟 **Cover Art** and Amazing **Illustrations** by dear friend E.V. Sparrow, _ev@sparrow.world_
- 🛟 **Title Graphic Designer**, David Veliquette, _davidartist.com_
- 🛟 **Formatting,** Julie DeEtte Williams, typographer

Heartfelt thanks to all of you, my friends, for sharing your wisdom, editing helps and encouragement. I couldn't have finished without you...

Joseph Bentz, Ph.D., EV Sparrow, Dee Bailey, Elaine Faber, Sande Heaton, Ellen Cardwell, Suzi Kneedler, Debbie Mullin, Terri Wildon, Dr. Jean M. Neill, Tracey Voss, David Veliquette, Sarah James, Cameron Brown, Sean Aspinall, David Aspinall, Sue Geranen, and...the husby of my heart, Steve <3

Dedicated to all the singles

Dating and waiting to meet your someone special

...Love will bloom again.
God is with you, always.

But hope that is seen is no hope at all. Who hopes for what he already has? But if we hope for what we do not yet have, we wait for it patiently. (Romans 8:24–25)

Table of Contents

Foreword by the Author

At age twenty-five, I was working as a hospital nurse and in my first serious relationship unsure if we should be pursuing marriage. I had been walking with the Lord since age seventeen, yet, I felt confused about the next stage in our dating relationship.

I asked God for direction. He gave me a simple rowboat analogy to identify the stages of the journey. Were we ready for the next step? Were we growing together or growing apart in God's will?

I hope this helps you identify:

1. What stage you are at in your relationship

2. Whether there is a future together

Note from Dee—Text in the circles or squares representing dialogue in the metaphor are hypothetical, not necessarily indicative of the caricatures representing Zach or Sarah. For example, the woman may be more logical or linear than the man or the man may want to proceed quicker in the relationship. However, usually opposites attract so the differences will be there regardless.

Speedboat—*Dating with Sexual Integrity vs Shortcut to Sex* is not in the metaphor but follows the Rocky Boat stage in the book.

Marriage Myth Busters—T/F expectations are at the end.

Each stage in this book will be defined using stories and Scriptures, my own experiences, and those of friends and acquaintances, plus information that bridges understanding the differences couples encounter.

- *The Dock*—the value of faith and knowing yourself
- *Dancing on the Dock*—meeting, acquaintance to friendship
- *The Relationship Boat*—is this a dating possibility?
- *The Talk*—the risk of connection and opening your heart to a dating relationship
- *The Rocky Boat*—balancing schedules and new emotions
- *The Speedboat*—dating with integrity vs shortcut to sex
- *Row the Boat, Gently*—growing together and communication skills
- *The Rapids*—navigating challenges as a team and making a crucial decision (Is this the person to share your love and future?)
- *He Leads Me Beside Quiet Waters*—trusting God's leading and finding peace in the final direction of a relationship

THE DATING DOCK METAPHOR
A Journey of the Heart

We are created to love and be loved by God and others for relationship.

THE DOCK—Who We Are, Where We Live

Know Yourself before You Add Another

Healthy relationships *begin when you embrace the value God gives you and others*. Only then can you truly love and be loved as God intends.

We each need a **Docking Place, a spiritual center** where *God meets our needs* through His Word, prayer and hope. The rhythm of nature—sunsets, tides, and seasonal changes, assures us of order and His Divine presence.

- Alone at the Docking Place, we reflect on opportunities, challenges, decisions and outcomes. *We realize God's love and peace* as we process feelings and thoughts in prayer and exercise trust, calm confidence in Him.

- When we know ourselves it brings balance to our interactions with others. Maturity and wisdom bring perspective. Patience enables us to persevere through storms, and celebrate life daily by learning to be content and grateful.

DANCING ON THE DOCK—The Meeting Place

> Sarah's a great girl. I'm attracted to her.

> Zach's fun to be around.

Where the Relationship Starts

The Opportunity—Social settings, conversations, activities, and invitations **create a connection**...interest sparks. Zach and Sarah are impressed.

"Zach seems to be serious about his faith."

"Sarah seems to be walking with the Lord."

Dancing is fun and easy for Sarah and Zach. They move in sync through changes in the rhythm and tempo of the music.

THE RELATIONSHIP BOAT—Is This a Potential Dating Relationship?

Zach begins to single out Sarah. As they spend time alone together and feel comfortable—as they share life—the *relationship boat* appears. Texts and calls increase...

Sarah wonders, "Does this mean he likes me? Is he just hanging out?"

Zach's conflicted. "Should I pay for her meal or will that make her feel pressure?"

The boat bumps against the pilings. Zach and Sarah feel the pounding of possibility. Friends ask if they will get in the boat.

Zach feels vulnerable. Sarah doesn't want to be hurt. Each is afraid of losing their friendship.

- Many friendships float in confusion waiting to see what will happen, wondering if they should talk.
- Both may watch the boat drift away—if they are indecisive or fearful. As time goes by feelings of resentment may surface in Sarah and Zach may feel bewildered. Awkwardness replaces the ease once felt in their friendship.
- The tension between hope and excitement or disappointment and loss is only resolved when each takes the risk to communicate.

The Talk—
The Risk of Connection

It takes courage...

to disclose feelings when the other person's feelings are unknown.

"I don't want to hang out with anyone else but you"

Zach realizes it's important to communicate his intentions after hanging out awhile. Zach waits for the right time. He hopes Sarah will at least agree to team up for a trial run.

THE ROCKY BOAT—

Adding Another

Adjusting "I" to "we"

Which foot do I put in first?

Feels a bit unsettling

Zach takes a leap of faith and suggests they both try rowing the boat. He offers a steady hand.

- Sarah agrees and steps into the boat, confident God will guide them. No matter the outcome, she hopes to grow as a person, and to treat Zach well.
- They both understand initial adjustments will have to be made in their schedules and decisions. Feelings can be unsettling with sleep and routines disrupted by the Rocky Boat.

Excited to be together, they each try to be considerate of each other.

ROW YOUR BOAT GENTLY—Consistent, Caring, Kind

Communication Moves the Boat Forward

How can two row together unless they agree?" (Amos 3:3 paraphrase)

"Faster to the left!"

"Slower to the right?"

- Are they rowing in the same direction, aware and responsive to each other, or creating *resistance*, paddling independently?
- Is one rowing faster than the other, causing the boat to circle? The **boat can only move as fast as the slowest rower.** Zach and Sarah are learning to listen and respect each other.

Zach thinks, "I'm not definite about my feelings. If I spend more time with her, hopefully, God will show me what to do."

Sarah wonders, "Could there be potential? What are his intentions?"

- Should they return to the dock and leave the boat? Are they able to communicate during a simple row across a smooth lake or are they out-of-sync?
- Are they bonding and enjoying each other's company? Zach and Sarah *are making headway*. They are ready to kayak.

THE RAPIDS—

The Challenging and Unseen

What were you thinking?

We need to get ready for the next rapid.

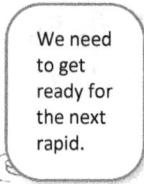

If we walk in the light as He
is in the light we have fellowship with one another (1 John 1:7)

Unexpectedly, the smooth waters of the lake surge into rapids. They abandon the rowboat and jump into a kayak. Open communication, quicker response and feedback are crucial. Zach and Sarah each pray and seek counsel.

Tensions rise as they dodge loose logs in turbulent waters. Their families notice difficulties. A storm rages. They nearly capsize.

- Zach doubts his abilities and begins to lose composure. Sarah is fearful her future is at risk and questions why she got in the kayak. They pray together.
- Zach and Sarah have discovered how they work as a team. The rapids behind them, they have gained personal insight and learned better how to resolve conflict.

Zach—Was this a test of our ability to work as a team? Are Sarah's questions resistance?

Sarah—Was this a warning of how difficult it is for us to work as a team? I don't understand Zach's leadership style...

HE LEADS ME BESIDE QUIET WATERS—

The Point of Decision

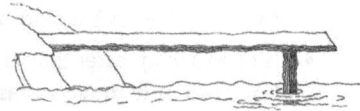

"Whew, God helped us through."

And restores my soul (Psalm 23:2–3)

Grateful for the growth and adventure Sarah and Zach relax and reflect. To step into a future together they must each **add** something to the other's life.

They pray for wisdom and guidance realizing they **must both be convinced** if their God-given destiny is to continue into marriage...or return to the dock and the dance.

INTRODUCTION

The Dating Dock

A Journey of the Heart

One day at a medical conference, an 18-year-old student sat next to me.

"What are you planning to do this summer?" I asked.

"I want to practice my trumpet and meet a girl!" He grinned from ear to ear.

The next week at a coffee shop, a college barista confided his relationship had ended abruptly as he slid me a bagel over the deli counter.

"How was your break up?" The question escaped as I handed him a dollar.

"Horrible. Relationships suck. I'm staying single." He rolled his eyes.

It doesn't take long to give up—feel unable to start or sustain a relationship. We begin hopeful and eager. If romantic-based friendships end with broken hearts from grief or rejection, we can feel sad, wounded or angry. Even with God in our lives. Even with loving family and friends. But feelings can heal and perspectives change.

God designed romance with the introduction of Eve to Adam in Paradise. It is a natural God-given instinct to desire a lifelong companion.

This book is designed to help you navigate the dating process. Read it with an open mind and open heart and may God bless your dating adventures.

THE DOCK
Who We Are, Where We Live, Our Docking Place

Know Yourself, Before
You Add Another

Master, Mission, Mate ~ The best time to think about meeting a lifelong friend and choosing a mate is after you have chosen your Master, realize your gifts and know your strengths and weaknesses.

Master ~ Jesus gave us the greatest commandment

> Love the Lord your God with all your heart, with all your soul with all your mind and with all your strength. The second is this: 'Love your neighbor as yourself.' There is no commandment greater than these. (Mark 12:30–31)

Jesus Christ loves you unconditionally and died for you. Are you able to receive the love, forgiveness and acceptance of your Creator? When He lives in your heart, you value yourself—and have His love to give to others. We know we are loved, forgiven and free of the past because we are—

> **Loved** ~ God demonstrates His own love toward us in this: While we were still sinners, Christ died for us. (Romans 5:8)

> **Forgiven** ~ If we confess our sins, He is faithful and just and will forgive us our sins and purify us from all unrighteousness. (1 John 1:9)

> **Free** ~ Therefore, if anyone is in Christ, he is a new creation; the old has gone, the new has come! (2 Corinthians 5:17)

Mission ~ We each have been given talents and gifts

For we are God's workmanship, created in Christ Jesus to do good works which God prepared in advance for us to do. (Ephesians 2:10)

> *When we know who we are, what we want, and where we are going, we can discover and experience a better match.*

❑ How can we apply this verse to our self-doubts?
God has not given us a spirit of fear, but of power, love, and a sound mind. (2 Timothy 1:7)

When we live to please God, people's approval comes second.

> *That you may walk worthy of the Lord, fully pleasing Him, being fruitful in every good work and increasing in the knowledge of God. (Colossians 1:10)*

• God will identify and bring good people into your life. Invest in yourself for a better you and to be a more positive influence for your friends.

> *Flee also youthful lusts; but pursue righteousness, faith, love, peace with those who call on the Lord out of a pure heart. (2 Timothy 2:22)*

"How do you know what God wants you to do with your life?" A friend asked her pastor one day.

He smiled. "You follow the love that springs up in your heart."

❑ What do you feel passionate about? What holds your interest over other activities or pursuits?

Remain in me, and I will remain in you. No branch can bear fruit by itself; it must remain in the vine. Neither can you bear fruit unless you remain in me.

I am the vine; you are the branches. If a man remains in me and I in him, he will bear much fruit. Apart from me, you can do nothing...As the Father has loved me, so have I loved you. Now remain in my love. (John 15:4-5, 9)

A calling is a gift to us from God that our nature responds to and our spirit rejoices in.

It is where our heart and passions lie.

When we use our gift, God is pleased. We feel purpose, and others feel valued. ~ Dee Aspin

---

Our Docking Place

We nourish our soul when we spend time with God to receive His love.

Meditating on the Word of God and praying with trust, releases anxiety and strengthens our spiritual core.

We become spiritually strong, by daily time with Jesus, the Bible and prayer

---

❑ Sometimes it helps to have a meeting place with Jesus. A chair, a table, a hiking path, even a coffee shop or an extended beach day. What are some ways you can be intentional and creative about spending time with God?

One morning at the hospital a patient in a painful relationship began to cry as I spoke of God's love for her.

She blurted out, "I have been feeding my body and starving my soul. I haven't been praying or reading my Bible."

Only our Creator can give us life.

We get life from God to share with others.
If we try to get life from others and share it with God...
our boat will sink.

Mate ~ Become the kind of person you would want to marry

Look to God
Help each other

At nineteen, I made a firm decision. A boyfriend I was very attracted to returned home from Easter break and hinted at a proposal. Early in our relationship he stated, "Don't bring the Bible out. I don't want to read it."

Now, he reasoned, "You believe in God and I don't. We will balance each other out." Although sad, I resolved without regret, to date only believers in the future.

GOD

**The closer we each
grow to God...the closer
we can grow to one another
in our relationship**

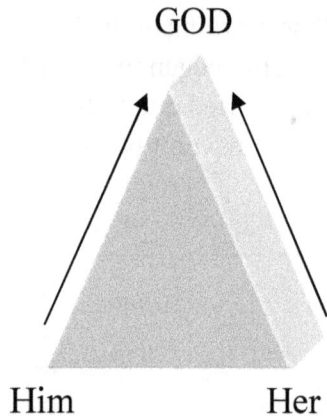

Him   Her

Through the seasons of life, the Bible compares the benefits of trusting God in hard times with the pitfalls of leaning on a person.

❏ Read *Jeremiah 17:5-8*. Give examples how you or someone you know has found this true.

The Past Unresolved is the Present

❏ What prevents us from moving forward in relationships?

Sometimes, unresolved issues from emotional wounds parallel physical injury to our body. Pain symptoms from nerve damage in our bodies range from high sensitivity to numbness.

Trauma to emotions range from defensive and highly sensitive responses to withdrawal, a lack of interest or an inability to discern what we are feeling.

When working pre-op surgery, I once asked a 5-year-old patient to choose one of five faces on a chart ranging from happy to sad so I could document how he described his feelings. He kept his index finger planted on the first face with the happy grin. "Are you sure that's the one?" Tears streamed down his cheeks as his lip quivered in fear. He nodded his head yes. He was obviously in distress, but couldn't express his true emotions.

- When we are able to identify the effect actions or words have upon us, we are in a position to communicate with honesty. In the safety of talking to God, we begin to gain understanding.

- God, our Creator and *only* true *Soulmate* designed marriage for the wonderful friendship, connection and support a lifelong loyal companion, a *Helpmate,* brings to us.

  And the Lord God said, "It is not good for man to be alone; I will make him a helper comparable to him..."
  Then the rib which the Lord God had taken from the man He made into a woman, and He brought her to the man. (Genesis 2:18, 22 NKJV)

At 23 Gabriella wondered if she would have met her mate if she hadn't left home to attend an East Coast university. Another friend was getting married and she was flying home to be in another wedding.

> *Waiting is part of the answer.*
>
> *Time is your friend.*

Again, a bridesmaid at 26, Gabriella waited with others in a wedding party for the groom's best man. He was riding cross-country on his motorcycle with a mission to make the wedding. Gabriella married the best man. She knew from the day he roared into her life he had the stamina to go a lifetime.

- No matter how long you have waited or how many prayers you have cried, God knows your heart. You can know and rely on His love for you. As you serve the Master of your life, may you trust Him for the mate He is preparing for you.

If anyone acknowledges that Jesus is the Son of God, God lives in Him and he in God. And so we know and rely on the love God has for us. (1 John 4:15–16)

A medical professional who married at 39 stated, "I never dated anyone longer than two weeks—that's all it took for me to know I wasn't interested." She and her husband, Bill, had traveled abroad with mutual friends who married after college. At the time, she had no interest in Bill other than friendship.

Then, after a broken engagement and a decade had passed, Bill returned to visit his hometown…and ran into her. Following a pleasant dinner together, he asked, "Could you be open to dating me?"

She smiled. "Yes."

DANCING ON THE DOCK

The Meeting Place—Where the Relationship Starts

The Effort to connect.
90% of life is just showing up

We are drawn to those who stir our minds or emotions.

Every person is drawn to particular music—from EDM and Alternative to country, rock/pop—the same way we are drawn to unique people. When we hear *our* music—we stop and listen. We are invited to the dance—time to step out of the sidelines and open the door for opportunity.

❑ What settings are you most likely to feel at-ease and natural?

outdoor activity	sporting event	friend's house
bar-b-q	theatre/movie	restaurant/coffee shop
church	single's groups	dances/concerts

Are you creating space in your life for others?

❑ Giving or receiving invitations to activities?

> *A smile, a glance*
>
> *So starts the dance...*
> *~ Dee Aspin*

❑ How can you create opportunities to pause for connection with others in your weekly schedule?

❑   What ways of connecting feel comfortable to initiate?

I asked Zach how he met Sarah.

"I met her at a church social." He grinned. "When I'm interested in someone—I watch them. If I like what I see, I smile at them…and take a chance. So I walked up to Sarah, smiled, and said, 'Hi, I'm Zach.' She smiled back."

We find opportunities to connect when we slow down and dance on the dock. If we meet someone we would like to get to know, whether introverts or extroverts who are shy with the opposite sex, anyone can learn to socialize more comfortably with practice. Start where you are, with the people around you, and maybe a little help from friends.

A friend shared, "I gave a party at our house and invited a guy my roommate was interested in."

❑   Are you looking in the right places? How can you change it up? Are there friends you can include?

❑   What new thing can you do that requires you to step out of your comfort zone without deviating from your moral compass?

Pre-requisites for Finding True Love

Brent told me he was really shy. "My friend, Shane, is my wingman. If I'm interested in a girl and she's surrounded by friends, we walk up together. Shane breaks the ice and asks her friends to dance and I will talk to the one I'm interested in. It helps a lot. I'm not so shy anymore."

- Love and accept yourself.

> *We all start at different places and we move at different paces.*

- You will be someone special to your someone special.

- Value those family and friends who already love *you* by not discounting their opinion. ☺

❏ Have you ever had a friend who was mesmerized over a person you found no particular interest in? What drew them to the person and how did you feel?

Attraction is in the eyes of the beholder. Whether hair or humor, skin color or body type, voice or scent, humor or hair style —we are who we are.

"Don't you hate your freckles?" After her friendly greeting, the stranger's question startled me.

"No, I don't even think about them." I stopped and turned to face her in the work corridor.

She furrowed her brows. "When I was a kid, other kids followed me home and teased me, 'You have mud on your face.' Later, a man I danced with in the evenings, saw me in broad daylight. He stared and smirked, 'What are those things on your face?' Freckles…I was so embarrassed."

She looked at me, eyes brimming. I felt incredulous and lucky. "All the guys I dated thought freckles were cute. My message was so different—it was, 'a face without freckles is like a night without stars.' Try saying that to yourself."

- Shake off rejection. There's *someone for everyone*.

- You are not unattractive or unlovable because the person you have eyes for…has eyes for someone else.

❏ Can you think of an instance where you or a friend struggled with rejection? How did you resolve your own feelings or help your friend sort through theirs?

Once at a singles function, I sulked over a guy who had given me a Valentine's card…and a dozen other girls in our church group. The following weekend we were all on a ski trip together. He skied all day with another gal and my expectations of "us" melted—I left the slopes early.

"Why waste time pining over a guy who doesn't like you?" A cheerful friend asked. "Just let it go. If they're not interested, that's their loss. I choose to like men who like me."

> *Relationships require Acceptance—knowing each other's strengths and weaknesses, dreams and goals, and being able and willing to align our lives together.*
>
> *Rejection is protection. It means the person is not a suitable fit to speak into our life, to offer a positive presence or to be close.*
>
> *Try not to take it personally. Timing is huge. A person may withdraw from pursuing a relationship due to unseen past or present circumstances—family or work obligations, distractions, even lacking solid direction from God.*

❑ Is there a time you felt intensely attracted to someone and then lost interest quickly? How come?

I was at a church singles gathering when the friend sitting next to me, a new believer, noticed a new girl walk in…and expressed he might ask her out.

"Why don't you wait a couple of weeks, and tell the Lord your feelings because you're just learning how to include Jesus in all areas of your life," I suggested.

> *Understand Infatuation?*
>
> *Passing intense attraction or chemistry without a foundation of friendship*

I'd already heard heart break stories from other girls who complained he came on strong and then 'dropped them' when he quickly lost interest.

We can't always avoid these situations but we can make it easier for others and ourselves, especially in groups that frequently gather.

Soon after he confided, "I'm so glad I didn't jump on my feelings. I've never prayed about feeling attracted to someone before. I'm glad I did. I'm not interested anymore."

❏ Have you heard of 'group dating'? What are the pros and cons and what are its limits?

Communication Creates Intimacy - Eye contact and physical presence, a voice, a text or email, words and, images, even emojis...sent with intention result in connection.

A twenty-something woman who was enjoying time with two men she met on dating sites commented, "I really don't like dating. It's so hard because even as you're getting to know someone, eventually you have to hurt people's feelings if you decide you're not interested. At my age, feelings are amplified because everyone's trying to meet a spouse."

❏ Describe an interaction where one conversation led to immediate connection and interest? Did you or the other person initiate a follow-up?

❏ Have you ever had a friendship or dating situation where the other person felt they connected well and you did not feel the same? What happened?

"I stopped online dating sites because I felt so rejected. I couldn't connect."

❏ Name some examples where online dating can work well and give some examples where it can hinder your growth?

In her twenties, Jen had spent months hanging out with Rick. His best friend, Ben, pulled her aside one day and said, "Jen, Rick is in love with you."

Jen laughed lightly, "I love him, too."

Ben looked concerned. "Jen, Rick loves you."

The reality lightbulb switched on in her head.

"I decided not to hang out with Rick anymore. He was so fun. We'd had a blast together. I would miss his friendship, but deep down inside I knew what I had to do—for his sake. It took Ben's intensity, looking at me straight in the eyes, to get to me. I've been very careful with guy friends ever since."

Hanging Out

A guy told a college student they were "hanging out."

Later she asked me, "What does that mean?"

Learn to protect your heart.

- The person knows where you are, knows your schedule and contacts you anytime.

- Text exchanges when you're out with others (inferring their importance to you...they are on your mind) sharing what you think about, things you see and hear.

- Going places with that person and including them with groups whether or not they are invited.

If you are initiating a hanging out relationship because you're looking for a commitment, you can be setting yourself up for disillusionment. Time together on *a regular basis can be a waste of your time* if you desire the potential of marriage and the other person doesn't.

If you are the regular recipient of someone else's attention, realize one of you can be creating an attachment and the other not—protect your heart from unintentional pain.

Sheila agreed to partner with a work acquaintance for weekly dance lessons. One evening as he twirled Sheila under his raised arm, he winked. "I'm not here for the dance. I'm here for you."

Sheila understood he wanted more than just a dance partner. After the series ended, they went separate ways—she was not interested.

> *Above all else, guard your heart, for it is the wellspring of life. (Proverbs 4:23 NIV)*

> *Above all else, guard your affections. For they influence everything else in your life. (Proverbs 4:23 TLB)*

❑ How do you define hanging out? Can you share any good or bad experiences from hanging out?

"How did you meet your husband, Ryan?" I asked the young woman telling us stories at class.

"I was on the treadmill at the gym and he was running next to me. We started talking and he made me laugh and he seemed really nice. What amazed me is just that morning I had been fighting with myself not to call someone who broke my heart. My sister warned me not to give in to the urge to call my ex. I'm so glad I didn't."

- Some friendships can turn into lifelong loves and others won't. You will never know if you don't get to know each other.

- If feelings grow on one side or the other, and you feel the bumping on your heart, like a boat against the pilings—it is time to verbalize what is happening inside you.

> Keep expectations down and go slow when getting to know someone.

"When I begin to like two girls at the same time, I choose one to get to know. I have tried dating two and it felt confusing. It works better for me to pick one and see what happens."

A young eligible pastor

This One is Special

In the dance of life we intersect

The young admin-assistant relayed, "My good friend kept bugging me to meet this great guy she knew, but I refused. I didn't have time. Then, one day she invited me to lunch and he was there. It was comfortable.

"We talked three hours. He invited me to coffee a few days later. After that, he would call every day at 8pm and I'd say, 'Okay, you have until 9pm.' I had school, work, and gym every morning—I was on a tight schedule. We would talk about what we read or learned every day and what we ate…

"We'd go to gatherings, and concerts. We were just friends. We never kissed.

"Then, he went out of town to check out a program at another college. His cell had died so he couldn't call that night. I missed his call. I wondered what happened and immediately, I felt so sad. The next day he called to say he was sorry…his phone had died.

"But, I realized how much he meant to me. So I waited until he came back in town and then invited him to dinner…so I could tell him I cared. He grinned. 'I know, we've been dating two years.' He was already committed to me all along…"

Even when we feel someone is special, they may not be where we are yet—

We may choose to wait before revealing our feelings. When we are ready—there are ways to step it up ☺

An engaged friend's fiancé told her after their relationship developed, "When we were getting to know each other, I didn't pay for meals because I didn't want to put pressure on you."

"Can I call you over Christmas break when you go home?" A handsome guy friend surprised me as we shared holiday plans with our families. That started a spark. I felt special.

> *Pace yourself… Lasting relationships are marathons—not sprints.*

❑ When you think someone is special, typically, how soon do you let them know? How do you let them know you are interested?

❑ What actions or words clue you in this person may be interested in you more than a friend?

THE RELATIONSHIP BOAT

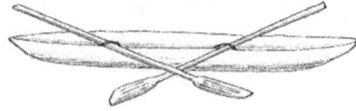

Is This a Potential Dating Relationship? Do You Feel What I Feel?

The first knocks at your heart are invisible but as real, as the feel of a boat bumping against pilings of a dock. The possibility of dating appears—the relationship boat *interrupts your thoughts*.

You may...

- **Feel your heart skip** when you see or hear that someone.

- **Find yourself scanning** emails or texts for a message.

- **Watching the door** to connect at meet-ups, or saving a seat, hoping...

Feelings ignored and unannounced by both, the boat will drift from the dock—and the opportunity for a relationship. Some prefer letting things settle, choosing to avoid embarrassment or fear by verbalizing their feelings.

- If one person *hangs out* to avoid loneliness and enjoy companionship without any intention of becoming emotionally involved, *the other can feel resentful*— especially if they've invested time and emotion, thinking the other had mutual feelings of possibility.

- *Awkwardness* or tension can begin to germinate when shared life experiences create fondness and burgeons hope...but nothing is expressed.

- *If feelings grow beyond friendship to attraction*, let the other person know so they can make responsible decisions in order to protect your heart or theirs.

- ***Withdrawal does not mean rejection***. No one wants to be accused of leading someone on—being a placeholder, if one friend feels romantic and the other doesn't.

The List

We all have a list, written or not, of the type of person we would love to spend forever with. Sometimes we don't know if there is potential with the person before us...

A counselor looked at me during a session and stated with a wry smile, "Well, you're not perfect either."

List what's important to you in a person you date.

Circle the non-negotiables.

> They aren't everything on our list. And maybe we aren't everything on theirs. ☺

1._____ 2._____

3._____ 4._____

5._____ 6._____

7._____ 8._____

9._____ 10._____

Major in the majors—minor in the minors

Everyone is a treasure chest. The longer we know someone, the more we discover what they're made of—what is valuable. We find the precious gems inside the outer wrapping. People are fragile, handle with care.

> *Focus on what's lasting—God centered? Virtue and valor. Kindness. Character remains. Clean and groomed? Clothes and hair change. Financial integrity is a lifestyle— good with a dime, good with a dollar. Jobs may be lost, Skills can be built. Positivity, humor and a smile adds...*

"See the red Miata—that's mine." The car serviceman pointed toward a sports coupe tucked in the parking lot as we walked to my car carrying a new windshield wiper.

"What's its name?" I joked.

"Jen," he smiled. "It's a girl. My girlfriend has a blue Miata the same year. Hers is a boy—Neiman."

"You sound like a great match!" I laughed.

"We are." He clasped his open palms together.

"Where did you meet?"

"I went to a local car-meet one weekend. I was standing at a car—she was standing next to me admiring the same car. We just started talking.

"Before she left, I asked for her number. We were friends for the first six months. She didn't want to date."

"What changed things?" I asked.

"I was determined. She was afraid if we dated it would spoil our friendship. But now, we've been dating as long as we were friends—six months. We're doing really good."

> *Relationship THEORUM*
> *1 whole person x 1 whole person*
> *=1 whole relationship*

The more Healthy (peaceful, God-centered, teachable, grounded) each person is, the better the relationship will be (communicative, active, mature, pleasant). **1 x 1 = 1**

The less Healthy (unstable, insecure, self-focused) each person is, the less satisfying the relationship will be (stagnant, stuck, immature, painful). **1 x ½ = ½**

- No one is perfect. Healthy people **want, not need**, a dating relationship. They value, develop and maintain meaningful family ties and friendships so they are not driven by loneliness to the wrong person. They are ready to choose the right person when they come along.

- We are all WIP's...works in progress.

❑ How does the following verse relay God's interest in your well-being and wholeness and in the person you are dating?

> ...*being confident of this, that he who began a good work in you will carry it on to completion until the day of Christ Jesus. (Philippians 1:6)*

❑ God called King David a man after his own heart. What motivated him?

> *May the words of my mouth and the meditation of my heart be pleasing in your sight, O Lord, my Rock and my Redeemer. (Psalms 19:14)*

❑ Think of one or two things you feel God may be nudging you to work on if you are in a relationship to be a better partner?

❑ If you are actively seeking to meet someone, what do you feel God may be leading you to work on now to better prepare for a relationship?

"THE TALK"
Taking the Risk to Connect

> *Risk being vulnerable and sharing your feelings.*

Stepping into the Boat Together—the Excitement and the Unknown

And the day came when the risk to stay the same became more painful than the risk to be vulnerable.

After another lunch together, I decided to see if my friend felt any change toward me—I had been thinking of him a lot. "Harry, I was wondering…I'd like to talk to you."

He gripped the counter, knuckles white, face flushed, "OH, NO!"

"No worries." I tucked my feelings and redirected the conversation.

❑ The potential of a long-term relationship is an underlying current.

> *Dating results in personal growth and maturity if we can push past our comfort zone.*

❑ If you don't risk anything you risk even more.

Before dating his wife, the speaker shared, "I couldn't move forward. We were great friends."

"What are you feeling?" the counselor had asked him.

"I don't want it to go bad and hurt her—and hurt me. I'm stuck."

22

- [ ] What are your expectations in a dating relationship—spiritually, emotionally, mentally, physically, socially, financially?

- [ ] What areas are absolutes, non-negotiables? What areas are negotiable—can be compromised?

- [ ] Good qualities in a person I'm seeking. Bad qualities I will avoid?

The shy thirty-something stated matter-of-fact after his marriage, "I was afraid of sharing feelings—but, I just kept pushing through the fear."

> *From the first "talk" relationships take W_O_R_K*
>
> *Willingness, Openness, Respect, Kindness...*
>
> *All positives*

- Communicating and understanding how to love and serve another.

- Determining what we want and need in a life-mate is a balance of both complementary and compatibility.

- [ ] Discuss the difference between complementary and compatibility using salt and pepper. Share some others.

Bret offered to look at my broken sprinklers. The next weekend he changed the oil in our cars. In the following weeks, we began mountain biking and playing tennis. Most of the time I had plans with girlfriends or group events on the weekend nights.

One day, Bret asked if I would like him to come by and pick me up to attend a church social event. *Hmmm. We would be attending together? Everyone would know we came together.* I had been enjoying his company and my feelings were growing…we needed to talk.

A few days later Bret and I were working out front when he asked again, "Would you like me to come by and pick you up for the dinner tonight?"

As we stood on my front lawn, I felt comfortable and this was my opportunity. "There's something I would like to say…if this is a good time? We have been hanging out six weeks now and this kind of feels like a date to me if you pick me up and we arrive together."

Quiet, he listened.

"You know how I don't like to volley a long time when we play tennis? I feel like it doesn't sharpen our skills, like diving into a set does. When we play to win or lose our game improves. The challenge brings growth. Similar to volleying on the tennis court, hanging out does not create attachment or sharpen communication skills the way a committed relationship does. I have hung out with men before and I don't want to do that anymore…unless we take the next step into a dating relationship."

Bret smiled. "I want to play a set."

> *Healthy relationships require two people talking about life and feelings with their hearts and heads in an atmosphere of acceptance and grace.*

"The Talk" may begin—

- "I enjoy your company. I'm not sure how I feel...would you consider..."

- "I'm willing to hang out awhile longer...if nothing changes, I'll know. We'll talk again."

❑ How long would you feel comfortable hanging out before moving on if you are the one who likes the other person? If you are the one who does not have the reciprocal feelings yet?

❑ What are other ways you have begun a "talk"?

- Someone once started a talk with, "I don't know if I will ever make much money, but I love my work."

- "I know I make more money...you are a hard worker, ethical and good at fixing things."

❑ What value can you bring to a relationship in terms of serving? Wisdom and encouragement? Help with house, yard, and car repairs? Computer or financial savvy? People skills and hospitality? Cooking? Organizing and planning—gatherings for hikes or potlucks? If one likes fancy dining can the other cook and create romantic dinners and home movie evenings?

❑ How do you feel about unequal education or earnings? How much difference does it make to you?

> *We can all struggle with feeling insecure and jealous. Acknowledging those feelings, praying and choosing not to act on them...frees us.*

"I haven't been in a relationship for years. I get too jealous."

❑ How do you handle jealous feelings?

❑ Have you been with someone who flirted with others when you were together? How did you feel and what did you do?

❑ If your date was acting jealous what could it look like?

❑ If you affirmed them more how did it help the problem?

❑ If you felt jealous and your date did not verbalize what they observed or valued in you, how would you approach them in an attempt to resolve your feelings? What would you say?

We affirm others when we speak words that build them up and validate their gifts and personality strengths, even when our significance comes from God. We are human. Jesus affirmed others—shepherds, women and children in a culture that didn't.

ROCKY BOAT
Adding Another
Balancing the Boat

#1 Rock my world with your presence and schedule.

What happens when two people step into a rowboat? It rocks. How much time do we invest? When do we connect?

"I can't talk to you every night on the phone until 1 a.m. I'm groggy for work in the morning," her new boyfriend sounded exasperated. "I need to switch things up." What was fun at first, wasn't anymore…at least for him.

"I can't say I didn't feel hurt," she smiled. "I looked forward to talking until midnight every night—but I've always been a night owl. He was trying to please me. I didn't realize it.

"Now we talk earlier for a much shorter amount of time, and we still see each other on Wednesdays and Saturdays."

You will discover your similarities and differences, where you can please and where yarou can't. How would you answer the following?

- News and political preference
- Perspectives about each other's friends or family
- Life habits—The Tidiness Factor-how clean are your living quarters or car
- Your favorite foods
- Your sleeping habits
- Preferred exercise or gym times
- Finances. Spender or saver
- Pets, type, number and their place in shared living quarters
- Desire for children

"We were friends and got along great so we had a talk." Steve frowned. "We tried dating a couple of weeks but it just didn't feel right. We talked again and both decided we will just stay friends."

#2 How much do we give feedback about the relationship?

It's exciting to be in a new relationship, but overly sharing feelings can produce pressure in a new relationship. Just experience life together and the journey as it unfolds. Talk as things arise. Give feedback as you need it or your significant other asks for it. Be aware. You may not want a deeper relationship. You are finding out more about the other person.

We were having dinner, and his face brightened. "I think it would be great to have five children."

I just stared and didn't say anything. He saw the shocked look on my face.

His voice lowered. "Four would be good, actually three children are okay, two would be fine…well, and I really don't think it matters."

I never said anything. But I learned something that contributed to my decision about our fledgling relationship. Our life desires were different.

#3 I feel like I don't know what I'm doing.

Every relationship has its own dynamics because when you put two different people together, you *never* get the same result. You can't compare this combination to past relationships. You have to find what works for *both* of you at this time of your lives by staying aware of *both* of your needs and wants.

> *New awareness—courage and humility to discuss differences, patience and diplomacy to deliver words kindly.*

"I wanted to stop and pick blackberries from the bushes during our beautiful kayak rental on the lake," Abby shared.

"He anticipated making it to a destination point and back in one hour.

"The conflicting wants turned our serene row into a surprise negotiation of rippling emotion…"

#4 Stay connected to others.

As you continue to learn about each other, remember, we give our lives to God to share with others. We share *most* with our significant other—not all. Every person who steps in the boat soon learns, *usually from a first voyage*—don't isolate yourself...or allow anyone to isolate you.

❏　What does it feel like to be isolated in a relationship?

"My first relationship, I dropped my friends and did everything with my boyfriend." Andrea winced. "When we broke up my friends were busy. I felt alone and lonely. I learned the hard way never to make that mistake again."

#5 Every relationship is a love laboratory.

We are free to experiment with how to love better...to improve communication, *to use humor* and *adapt.*

> DATING...two people attempting to connect with the possibility of a romantic relationship.

Fear and nervous jitters gripped me. I felt like I didn't know what I was doing. My obsessiveness to control could ruin this friendship. I had to work on trusting God—relax and focus on living in the moment.

- The boat stays balanced as we're calmed by Jesus, smack in the center of the boat with us.

- Don't invest yourself too quickly. Allow the relationship to unfold in the natural course of time.

- Jesus' voice and guidance is simple. Follow Him daily.

- Row in the light, as He is in the light.

> *In healthy dating, each will grow in their ability to communicate feelings, ideas, dreams and desires.*
>
> *If each feels satisfied and validated as individuals, they may transition to potential life partners, evidenced by their present schedules and future plans together.*

By your endurance you will gain your lives. (Luke 21:19 ESV)

Greek—(*hupomone*)—cheerful or hopeful endurance, constancy, patient continuance

- Jesus' voice seems distant when drowned by doubts—when we fear loss before we've even begun a new journey of our heart. Often, we've waited for the opportunity to have someone special in our lives.

- We can learn to relax when we thank God for each day as it comes, keep loving Him first and living in the present.

The strength and skill a rowboat requires are needed as soon as we push off the dock. It relies on a partner's unknown abilities which can play on emotions if the lake looks as wide as an ocean.

The longer two grasp at opposing oars deciding how to forge the journey ahead, while failing to convey requests and responses well—the more inviting the detour—especially, if the chemistry is strong.

THE SPEEDBOAT
Dating with Integrity vs. Shortcut to Sex

In-FAST-uation =

THE POWER OF TEMPTATION, EXCITEMENT AND PLEASURE

> *Moses chose to be mistreated along with the people of God rather than to enjoy the pleasures of sin for a short time. (Hebrews 10:25 NIV)*

A smooth, shiny **speedboat** is docked in the harbor ready to reach the deep...in seconds. A sly seaman beckons tense couples to discard the long row ahead, and slip off into the rush of immediate gratification...minus the Captain of their Salvation.

Forget the rowboat—let's climb into the speedboat.
Speedboats are great if you want intensity, the thrill of going fast—but speedboats need fuel to move forward. They can run out of gas quickly.

- ***Relationship boats*** depend on the skill of the oarsmen and communication to propel forward. People who have the skills to communicate, develop the perseverance to work together and adapt to the extreme adventure of difficult challenges in life and love

A friend stated, "When I was young if things got crazy and we would start arguing, I would just kiss my boyfriend really hard. It would distract him, and the problem would go away for a while."

- Sex is powerful and created by God as a beautiful expression of faithful love and intimacy reserved for marriage, even though the temptation exists.

- Outside of marriage, sex is a speedboat. For some, it is a comfortable delusion to skip the hard work of rowing.

Far from shore, if the boat runs out of fuel—you have to row the boat. God is not the pilot. The sensual smokescreen down, it may be a shock when we face each other in deep water—the boat is vulnerable to changing weather conditions and an unprepared crew.

> *The Decision to reserve the gift of intimacy for your mate is made before the date.*

Once I boarded a sailboat in the Santa Cruz harbor with a good friend. We had been invited for a sail around the bay.

We cautiously stepped down rickety steps into a knotty pine cabin where a sign greeted us below deck. "On this vessel, all marriages are conducted by the captain and limited to the duration of the voyage." I looked at my friend and whispered, "Let's get out of here."

Putting the past behind you, your decision now will plant seeds for a new future and reap benefits. As you initiate self-control and overcome temptation through God's strength as a single, you will build confidence in your ability to remain faithful in your marriage.

> *You are gifting your future mate with the exclusive privilege of knowing you as others cannot by reserving yourself to be cherished by a true love.*

A newlywed shared a memory of the second date with her husband.

"As the evening drew to a close we both lingered by his car. I didn't want him to kiss me and felt the urge to speak… 'I want to honor God in our relationship. I want purity. I have never had that, and it is what I feel God is calling me to.'

"I thought after I shared my conviction it would be over.

"He smiled and sounded relieved, 'I want that too.'"

It is God's will you should be holy; that you should avoid sexual immorality; that each of you should learn to control his own body in a way that is holy and honorable, not in passionate lust like those who do not know God; and in this matter no one should wrong his brother (sister) or take advantage of him (her).
(1 Thessalonians 4:3–4 paraphrase)

God's manual for relationships, the Bible, is loaded with tools for interpersonal relationships as God intended. From the wisdom of Proverbs in the Old Testament to Jesus's truth and insights in the New Testament, we are given an invitation to believe and receive His Spirit and become born-again children of God (John 3:7) loved, forgiven and free. We are encouraged to love others wisely and unselfishly.

- The will to follow Jesus, and draw upon His strength to live as He intended in our relationships, is possible as we trust and obey Him. We can trust He knows us because He loves us and made us. Romance was His idea since He created man and woman, Adam and Eve, in the Garden of Eden.

- The Biblical actions of love described in 1 Corinthians 13:7–10 are—patience, kindness, believing others have good intentions (not suspicious) not jealous, boastful or easily irritated, not keeping record of wrongs, able to hope and believe the best in someone, bear and endure their struggles...as we rely on God's infinite resource, not ourselves.

DRAWING THE LINES OF RESPECT

- Love chooses to do the highest and best for another's lasting good.

- Healthy relationships require emotional maturity and self-control.

God designed relationships to glide at the speed of rowboats so a team rhythm, able to survive the storms of life, could develop.

In adult relationships the foundation of trust is built on the confidence both desire to honor God and each other.

Our bodies are Temples of the Holy Spirit.

That is why I say to run from sex sin. No other sin affects the body as this one does. When you sin this sin it is against your own body. Haven't you yet learned that your body is the home of the Holy Spirit God gave you, and that he lives within you? Your own body does not belong to you. For God has bought you with a great price. So use every part of your body to give glory back to God, because He owns it. (1 Corinthians 6:18–20 TLB)

☐ What are some ways sexual sin affects our body? Our mind? Our spirit? Why would God place specific instructions and guidelines for sex if it is good?

"Sin," in Greek, literally means "missing the mark." It's like shooting an arrow at a bullseye and missing. Protective and wise, God details in Leviticus 18 when sex is harmful.

Sex is a gift to **reserve** for our true love and **preserve** within marriage with our faithful one.

- God created sex as a bond for a lifetime.

    Haven't you read, "He (Jesus) replied, "that at the beginning the Creator made them male and female, and said , 'For this reason a man will leave his father and mother and be united to his wife, and the two will become one flesh' so they are no longer two, but one. Therefore, what God has joined together, let man not separate. (Matthew 19:5-6)

Expressing Affection...expressing fondness and care.

Think how easily children take your hand or give a hug. Or a pet simply nuzzles against you.

After the speaker finished his presentation at a Christian singles conference, a vibrant discussion on celibacy followed the question, "How far can we go?"

One man answered, "I figure anything I would feel good about if Jesus were standing there. He sees anyway."

Another young professional shared what had worked for her since adolescence. "The body still responds the same, so I have always used the same camp rule as I did when I worked as a teen camp counselor—keep your clothes on. Boy's hands don't go where the girl's bathing suit is, and girl's hands don't go where the boy's bathing suit is."

A woman relayed, "I'm direct about my boundaries. I just say, 'My body is my ballpark and I make the rules.'"

A man stated, "I try to get to know someone. I don't like to kiss for a couple months, so my emotions don't get clouded."

- **Sex is like a firecracker** ~ Ignited feelings can turn sexual, like a firecracker which burns faster toward the fuel case. We must slow the intensity.
- **The law of diminishing returns** ~ The more we do, the more we want. *"There is a time to refrain from embracing." (Ecclesiastes 3:5)*
- **Time-outs** ~ Couples find ways to honor their commitment and avoid extended time alone. Stretching

periods between connecting, double-dating, group activities, bucket lists, serving together in ministry.

A Christian sister shared, "My boyfriend leaves my apartment after we watch a movie. He doesn't like to stay past midnight...to avoid temptation."

❑ Is there any situation you relate to now and can talk to Jesus about prayerfully? What is He saying to you? Is there a need for a conversation with the person you're dating?

> *We learn a lot about ourselves and others in how we handle temptation. Sexual purity by a single believer is an indicator of their commitment to Christ.*

Blessed is the man who endures temptation, for when he is tried he will receive the will receive the crown of life, which the Lord has promised to them that love Him. (James 1:12 KJV)

Accountability helps us walk the walk.

❑ What is the value of an accountability partner? If you are dating, who could you trust to question you with good intent? What would be the qualities of the person you ask?

❑ How can we be our own worst enemy in the area of temptation? See James 1:13–15

THE TRUTH ABOUT SEX

It can hurt us...even if we are two consenting adults.

The world we live in treats sex as if we can separate our physical body from our emotions. Sex is much more than a simple act to fulfill a physical drive as noted in *The Invisible Bond by Barbara Wilson*. Two hormones, oxytocin and dopamine, released during sex seal a bond of oneness and pleasure to glue two souls together.

The physical intimacy created by the closest physical bonding a abandonment and protection from the diseases inherent with multiple partners. Biblical teaching has not changed because creation has not changed.

In The Act of two becoming one, two souls give to each other part of themselves.

- During the act of sex, an intimate part of each person is given and taken. Random partners *disable the superglue* of sex God created to seal two souls. Feelings associated with the act of sexual intimacy to create love and bonding are lost, much like overused Velcro ripped and limp with every break up or meaningless alliance.

> *Sex outside of marriage brings guilt or conviction to a Christian walking close to the Lord.*

- The beautiful act of sex without love becomes a physical act devoid of the feeling and emotional connectedness it was meant to deliver. "Sex doesn't mean anything" results.

It's easier to love and leave, lacking the vows to love each other for better or worse. A committed decision to love someone for a lifetime results from the sense of God's leading—especially when we truly realize the energy it takes to build a healthy relationship.

If you were left, you can feel rejected and ashamed. If you leave when the pleasure is over, you may have scarred someone and feel remorse.

- **The internal and spiritual damage** to our psyche is partly from the inability to form relationships by using sex.

- **Sex was never created to launch a relationship**. It was designed to bring pleasure and expression to marriage.

- **God wants us to have a pure conscience**, to enjoy each other because we are faithful to Him and good for each other.

A newly-married man confided, "I wish I hadn't slept with other women before. I love my wife, but now I have had to deal with flashbacks. God gives us wise counsel to protect us. He knows how we were made."

Have you been desensitized to touch?

- Common if you have been manipulated by individuals, the culture or forced into unwanted or frequent sexual encounters. You are not alone. Hope exists for new beginnings. There's always second chances for a fresh start and positive dating experiences—as Jesus leads the way.

The Holy Spirit wants to comfort and counsel you through your dating relationship. Include Him in your feelings, and struggles, the good, the bad and the ugly.

❑ How do the following passages strengthen and comfort you?

Psalm 145:8, 9, 14

> *v. 8 The Lord is gracious and full of compassion; slow to anger and rich in love.*

> *v. 9 The Lord is good to all; His tender mercies are over all his works (KJV). He has compassion on all He has made (NIV)*

> *v. 14 The Lord upholds all those who fall and lifts up all who are bowed down.*

Psalm 147:3

> *He heals the brokenhearted and binds up their wounds.*

❑ Journal any verses that correct your view of God and help you understand His love for you.

If you have been fettered with shame or guilt, receive His kindness and help by allowing yourself to change. Be the new you. Value and respect yourself by each small step toward dignity. Tell someone you trust.

LOVE VS. LUST

LOVE requires loyalty and deep affection. When the desire is met to love and be loved by another unconditionally in spite of knowing each other's flaws—we experience intimacy.

- We feel attached and cared for which brings us peace when we give and receive real love.

- When we love as God intended, a rich spiritual, mental, emotional and physical closeness ***provides contentment and satisfaction that deepens over time.***

❑ Give an example of a couple you know who exhibit true love. What makes them outstanding?

LUST is a strong desire that can only be filled temporarily.

- A lustful relationship is driven by the pleasure passion gives. Consideration is not given the other person to feel special or loved.

- Lust wants what it wants when it wants it...which creates a problem resolving differences.

- Lust grows restless in proportion to time, needing more, different and better. A relationship built on lust cannot provide enduring satisfaction.

❑ The Bible refers to three areas of life that unchecked become lusts. What are they? Read 1 John 2:16 below. Give examples where you have seen this occur?

> Do not love or cherish the world or the things that are in the world. If anyone loves the world, love for the Father is not in Him. For all that is in the world, the lust of the flesh (craving for sensual gratification) and the lust of the eyes (greedy longings of the mind) and the pride of life (assurance in one's own resources or in the stability of earthly things)—these do not come from the Father but are from the world (itself).
>
> And the world passes away and disappears and with it the forbidden cravings (the passionate desires, the lusts) of it; but he who does the will of God and carries out His purposes in his life abides (remains) forever.
> (1 John 2:16–17 AMP)

LOVE stands the test of time.

Anything of value can be copied, even "love" and "faith" within a person. God tests us, Satan tempts us. A counterfeit bill must be held in the light and put through a scan to check it. In the same way, it is hard to determine genuine faith at a distance. What's underneath, virtue or vice, lust or love? One test—Love can wait. Lust can't.

❑ How can you tell if a man is a wolf in sheep's clothing? (Matthew 7:15–17 and 2 Timothy 3:13)

❑ If a woman is seductive and cunning? (Proverbs 7:17–27)

❑ Why would God require and command His people to control their bodies before marriage? (Matthew 5:27–28)

❑ What value does this add to trust and fidelity within marriage? (Romans 13:13–14)

How Do We Flee Lust?

Pray to Jesus, our merciful and faithful High Priest before God, who understands our weakness. For since he himself has now been through suffering and temptation, he knows what it is like when we suffer and are tempted, and he is wonderfully able to help us. (Hebrews 2:18 TLB)

Don't focus on the temptation in the midst of temptation. Dwell on what's right, honorable, noble, and true. (Philippians 4:8)

- **Turn our eyes** away from the source. *I made a covenant with my eyes not to look lustfully at... (Job 31:1)*

"Have you heard the term **bounce**?" Puzzled, I looked at the single Christian woman and shook my head.

"This morning at the gym a very good looking man was working out ten feet in front of me. Suddenly, he pulled off his shirt! *Oh my word, Lord...I don't need this in my current state!* I needed to look elsewhere—so I *bounced* my eyes somewhere else. Bounce...bounce..." ☺

- **Turn our thoughts** to Christ. Push past impure magazines, images, and look to Jesus... (Hebrews 12:2)

- **Find the door** of escape. "Lord, what do you want me to do, now, instead?"

- **The Holy Spirit gives us power** to overcome. *No temptation has seized you that is not common to man, but God is faithful to His Word... He can be trusted not to let you be tested beyond your power to endure... He will always provide a way of escape that you may bear up under it. (1 Corinthians 10:13 paraphrase)*

> "A Temptation is an opportunity to do the right thing."
> ~ Rick Warren

A story is told of Saint Augustine, an early believer, who met Christ after many years of living a wild life.

One day when he passed a woman on the street he had once been with. She yelled out, "Augustine, it's me!"

He answered, "That's why I'm running. It's not me."

No longer dominated and defined by sin, but a new man defined by Christ, his past was buried at the cross where Christ died to forgive him and set him free...redeemed and new.

"No matter what our past, Christ died for that sin so we don't have to keep bringing it up." ~ Pastor Rich Sherman

THE BATTLE IN THE MIND

The Enemy's Strategy...Satan, the "deceiver."

Our Accuser. Satan targets our mind—intent to bullseye our emotions with fiery darts of doubt, fear, discouragement, anger, jealousy, hatred and lust—He shoots it all. We must extinguish the darts and throw them back.

> *Resist the devil and he will flee...come near to God, He will come near to you. (James 4:8)*

Master of Magnification. Satan feeds on our fear. Molehills look like mountains. Pray for faith.

The Opportunist. Satan is like a wolf who attacks the lone, the weak and the young sheep. Stay connected to others, and close to Jesus.

"Our discipleship should remind people that what God most cherishes, the devil most hates. We shouldn't be surprised by the schemes of the evil one. If sex is as profound, powerful, pleasurable, and protected as God's word says it is, it's no wonder that Satan would want to destroy it and make it the very opposite--meaningless, painful, alienating, and full of regret." Evangelizing in a World Drowning in Sexual Problems, by Randy Newman, https://www.biblestudytools.com/blogs/randy-newman/evangelizing-in-a-world-drowning-in-sexual-problems.html

> *Jesus said, 'If you hold to my teaching, you are really my disciples. Then you will know the truth, and the truth will set you free..." (John 8:32)*

- **Human beings are comprised of the Body, Soul, and Spirit.** The Spirit is where we commune with God. Our body helps us relate to the physical world. Our **Soul** (heart) is our distinct nature and personality. It's composed of 4 parts—**our mind** (thoughts), **will** (ambitions), **emotion** (feelings), and **conscience** (moral compass). ~ *Priscilla Shirer, Armor of God, p 71*

- **Good guilt** is specific. We act or think against our *conscience* and we are prompted by the Holy Spirit to ask forgiveness for an identified sin and take the right path. God is faithful and just to forgive our sins. Our relationship with God is restored and our Spirit, where we commune with Him, is free again. Guilt in Greek means, "bound by, to owe, to be indebted."

If we confess our sins He is faithful and just to forgive us our sin and to cleanse us from all unrighteousness. (1 John 1:9 KJV)

- **False guilt** is a vague sense we've missed something. "We take responsibility for people or things outside of our control and suffer self-condemnation because we can't change the outcome. The self-condemnation interrupts our walk with God. We always feel judged" (*Charles Stanley*). Enemy lies rip through our heart and "guilt feelings" plague us—even with confession. The answer is to recognize the lie and let go.

> "Confession leads to grace... not disgrace."
> ~ Rick Warren

And let the peace of Christ rule in your heart. (Colossian 3:15 RSV)

❏ What is one way to meet the goal of sexual purity according to 2 Timothy 2:22 below?

Run from anything that gives you the evil thoughts young men often have, but stay close to anything that makes you want to do right. Have faith and love, and enjoy the companionship of those who love the Lord and have pure hearts... (TLB)

❏ Where can you go this week to find those like-minded peers? What place is best to avoid?

There was a time I felt particularly vulnerable to lust. It seemed all day long I battled sudden lewd images that slid into my thoughts. I resisted the enemy by deflecting the ideas he hurled my direction while asking God for a clean mind and heart.

> "You cannot keep birds from flying over your head, but you can keep them from building a nest in your hair." ~ Martin Luther

By the end of the day I felt guilty, even though most of the time I didn't let the birds land, so to speak. When I lingered on a thought, I immediately asked God's forgiveness.

Yet, I felt defeated *until* an older Christian warned me not to trust unstable feelings. "Our Accuser exploits them," she said. "When we fight temptation it is wearing. Even when we conquer the temptation, just the fact we've dealt with it repeatedly contributes to guilty feelings."

❏ How does the verse below set us free from unrelenting feelings of failure and guilt?

> *This, then is how we know that we belong to the truth, and how we set our hearts at rest in His presence whenever our hearts condemn us. For God is greater than our hearts, and He knows everything. (1 John 3:19–20)*

Talking—we can work it out.

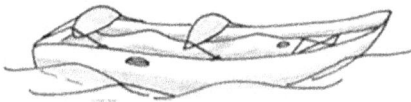

Talk to God and spill your heart, emotions and secrets. He hears and counsels what is right.

*Trust in Him at all times, you people; Pour out your heart
before Him; God is a refuge for us. (Psalm 62:8)*

❑ Find a safe/wise person, pastor, counselor to confess your
deed or thoughts to pray with and seek counsel.

*He who covers his sins will not prosper, but whoever
confesses and forsakes them will have mercy. (Pr. 28:13)*

❑ Write a brief prayer to God asking for His help.

SEXUAL HEALING

The Lies that—"Sex doesn't mean anything" and "My
body is not valuable"—result from...

- Giving our bodies away to others, sharing
  closeness and intimacy designed for lifetime
  lovers.

- Abusers–Control of our bodies has been
  stolen, overtaken or used by broken people
  controlled by destructive or deceitful behavior.

- People created in God's image are displayed devoid of
  spirit or emotion and reduced to bodies used for
  seduction and marketing.

- An unreal world, pornography, where a person lusts after
  images of people, they do not and cannot know. Bodies
  are viewed absent of emotional feeling or deep affection,
  strictly to fill the pleasure of the voyeur.

**God
is
a
Healer.**

> *If you have a sexual addiction...if your mind and emotions are being assaulted via pornography because of your own doing or because you were violated through another person's damaged psyche, you are not alone.*

I bless the holy name of God with all my heart. Yes, I will bless the Lord and not forget the glorious things he does for me. He forgives all my sins. He heals me. He ransoms me from hell. He surrounds me with loving kindness and tender mercies. He fills my life with good things! My youth is renewed like the eagle's! (Psalm 103:2–3 TLB)

- Jesus rescues us from darkness and guides us into the kingdom of light and hope. (Colossians 1:12-14)

- He binds open, festering wounds from our past. (Psalm 147:3)

- Jesus gripped Peter's hand, rescuing him from sinking. The mental weights of fear and doubt, Peter's faith walk-on-water as he tried to follow Christ. When we call for help Jesus reaches out His hand—immediately.

- He forgives and directs. He will provide a path to safety and safe people. He directs, "Go and sin no more."

RESOURCES FOR HEALING

Celebrate Recovery Programs are Biblically-based, recovery programs at churches in many cities for sexual addictions, co-dependents and more. Help is taught in building fences, or boundaries around lives. Resources are available and tools for freedom from damaged emotions. Just google, "celebrate recovery program." In addition, see below.

American Association of Christian Counselors ~ https://www.aacc.net/

XXX Church ~ https://www.xxxchurch.com/ Help for couples, men, women, spouses, students / support groups, workshops, accountability software for monitoring, blocking content

Josh McDowell Ministry: Just 1 Click Away ~ https://www.josh.org/resources/just-1-click-away/

Beggar's Daughter ~ https://beggarsdaughter.com/ ministry dedicated to walking with women addicted to pornography

Internet Accountability and Software Programs

Covenant Eyes ~ http://www.covenanteyes.com/personal/

K9 Web Protection ~ http://www1.k9webprotection.com/

Net Nanny ~ https://www.netnanny.com/

> *If we confess our sins, he is faithful and just and will forgive us our sins and purify us from all unrighteousness. (1 John 1:9)*
>
> *Blessed is the man whose sin the Lord does not count against him and in whose spirit is no deceit. (Psalm 32:2)*

The Speedboat ran out of gas. Secrets are out. Back at the dock, one or both of you have new accountability in place, through a group, mentor, friends or pastor.

You must each decide between the rowboat and the dance on the dock...

- ❑ Is God leading you to begin again, this time in the rowboat, with Jesus centering you both?

> *Feelings come and feelings go and feelings are deceiving*
>
> *My warrant is the Word of God, it alone is worth believing...*
> ~ Martin Luther

❑ Are one or both of you leaning toward joining others at the dance on the dock until you regain your bearings?

The Rocky Boat settles. The couple is headed the same direction with the same intention—to stay sexually pure and honor God by honoring one another's bodies as belonging to God first.

❑ Fill in the following verse below: 1 Corinthians 6:19-20

Do you not _____ that your _____ is a

_____ of the _____, who is

_____ whom you have received from _____?

You are not _____; you were bought at a _____.

Therefore _____ God with your _____.

The water is tranquil. Hands to oars, each is ready to move forward—the rowing begins.

ROW YOUR BOAT, GENTLY

Consistent, Caring, Kind Communication Moves the Boat Forward

"How can two row together unless they agree?" (Amos 3:3 paraphrase)

As the Boat Settles, the Rowing Begins

- You've started a **journey of the heart** with someone special who will influence you this season of your life. You will grow and learn how to communicate better as you row together.

- Enjoy the scenery. Dance in the moments. No need to rush. Time is your friend.

Life has many facets.

Family, friends, work, school, church, hobbies.

> *You can only move as fast as the slowest person.*
> *~ Dee Aspin*

❑ How much time can you give to the relationship? A weeknight or two? Saturdays?

Are You Rowing Together?

- **Adjustments** ~ *Make polite requests.* "I see a rock jutting out, we need to shift gears," may not be enough. Don't **assume** your partner is aware what to do, or worse, judge they should know. "Please paddle faster on the right—I'll row from this side."

- **Listening and Responding ~** *Respond.* "I don't see anything"...isn't the best response. Rather, trust the credibility of your row mate. "Okay, it's *great you see it.* I'll row faster."

> *As issues arise, The BOAT WILL CIRCLE or halt if clear communication is ignored...*

- **Timing ~** *Honesty.* The speed of the boat, the relationship, can only move as fast as the slowest rower—the limits of their time, energy and emotions. "I *can't* row any faster."

- **Flooding ~** *Patience.* Too much talk about the relationship too soon, can waterlog the mind and sink the boat. A person may respond by distancing—jumping out of the boat for a solo swim—a pause.

Jake enjoyed Sarah's company, their Saturday morning runs and social times with friends. They liked the same activities and seemed to get along well. However, Jake's work demands including travel, had significantly increased.

He explained, "The same day I planned to tell Sarah I needed to pull back on our relationship for a while, she told me she wanted more time together and closeness. We stopped dating."

> *Pauses are part of a rowboat experience. They may be temporary or pre-empt the end of the journey.*

A pleasant row? Keep the focus simple, one stroke at a time. One movement forward is progress, and so is a mutually relaxing pause on the water. Trust God is guiding you today. Affirm each other as often as you can. "I really like being with you." *And say it with a smile!*

- The legendary research on communication by UCLA Professor, Dr. Albert Mehrabian, revealed...only 7% of communication is verbal—the literal meaning of words we use with one another. Non-verbal and visual cues *predominantly convey* true meaning. These are: **tone of voice, facial expression, gestures, posture, eye contact, movement, visual appearance...**

My boyfriend called and broke a date—he was sick. I asked to meet with him briefly the following week as I battled pain from familiar foes—insecurity and abandonment.

I question words and am slow to trust. It is important for me to talk in person. "Are you avoiding me because you feel trapped?"

Instantly, hurt clouded his face and tears sprang to his eyes. I knew he really had told me the truth. My pain dissolved before he said a word.

*Gently Row...***gentleness** is strength under control. Jesus exemplified gentleness.

- Women love a gentle man. God loves a gentle man. Jesus encouraged his disciples, "...learn from me, for I am gentle and humble in heart, and you will find rest for your soul." (Matthew 11:29)

- Men love a gentle woman. God loves a gentle woman.

  Your beauty should not come from outward adornment, fine clothes and braided hair...it should be that of your inner self, the unfading beauty of a gentle and quiet spirit (un-disturbed, un-disturbing) which is of great worth in God's sight. (1 Peter 3:3–4 paraphrase)

- Gentleness is a fruit of the spirit. We can yield our nature to the Holy Spirit and ask God to produce gentleness in us. Frustration expressed with empathy and delivered to a fragile heart softly like a Nerf ball, evokes a better result than a heart scathed by the pelt of an icy snowball.

One Saturday morning, I told my boyfriend, "We need to go for a walk and have some extended exercise." He hesitated and decided no. Later he said he wanted to and even planned to initiate something, active, but as soon as I said it in such a commanding way…he didn't want to. I felt so frustrated with him. He felt I wasn't asking him, but telling him. "It would be better to ask me, would you consider…"

The following Sunday at church with a longtime friend, the pastor announced a prayer meeting after the service.

"Oh good!" Excited, I turned to her, "We have to go."

Later, my friend confided that something inside her rebelled. "Even though initially I wanted to go and did, I really didn't want to after your strong prompt. It felt like I didn't have a choice."

"Did you feel controlled?" I asked.

"Yes," she said. "It's better to ask, 'Would you consider?'"

> *Would you consider?*
>
> *I wonder if you tried it this way…*

You can get your point across by whispering.

❑ Share an example of a difficult situation when someone's harsh delivery delayed a positive outcome and a time when someone's gentle approach produced good results.

❑ How does passivity and withholding opinions for the sake of peace affect a relationship?

Beware: Criticism → contempt[1]

Be: Grateful → respect

❑ How can you turn criticism to respect? What does God require of us?

- ***Do not repay anyone evil for evil. (Romans 12:17)***

The principle of giving a blessing for a curse is a spiritual fact, and conveyed by Scripture. When roommates or friends or family do annoying things or say hurtful words—instead of judgment and criticism—***Let go*** of rising resentment. Ask the Lord to help heal both of you.

- ***Do not think of yourself more highly than you ought. (Romans 12:3)***

A critical thought or bitter root starts as a seed—but if left untended it can dominate and obscure any view of virtue in the other—contempt planted, now thrives. Disgust prevails. We all have good, bad and ugly. We are all fully loved by God. We are each made in His image, equally loved and gifted.

- ***Do not be overcome with evil, but overcome evil with good. (Romans 12:21)***

We overcome when we...*stop rehearsing* the wrong. *Release* anger by forgiveness. *Review* the right and good virtues about the person. *Bring* God glory by asking for His help, honoring His Word. *Do something good* toward the person.

---

[1] Gottman, John, Ph.D., and Nan Silver (1999*) The Seven Principles for Making Marriage Work*, (pp. 27-31). Three Rivers Press, New York

BALANCING THE BOAT

Good team relationships require rowing in sync. Giving and receiving. Talking and listening, gently. Responding correctly to sensible words. Check your approach. Is the delivery. Soft?

- Ask for what you need. Request, not demand. No one reads minds. Be patient. You change slowly, too. Trials and tests are good for relationships. Time reveals maturity and humility.

> *Check your approach.*
>
> *Think before you speak.*
>
> *Is the delivery soft?*

- Guard against selfishness or giving too much.

❑ Are you giving too much or too little? Of time, emotions, gifts? Are you splitting costs for outings? Meals? Gas? There are ways to balance purchases by acts of service if one doesn't have cash. Cooking meals, fixing pc glitches or broken faucets, doing research, arranging social events...

❑ If you felt you were bearing the brunt of the rowing, what would you do? How long would you continue? What does an imbalanced relationship feel like?

Encourage daily. *The tongue has the power of life and death... (Proverbs 18:21)*

- Speak the truth in love. Be respectful. Disrespect destroys relationships.
- Agree to disagree by simply stating, "That's your opinion."

❑ Tell your partner an attribute you appreciate about them and thank God for their uniqueness.

Analytical Personalities

"My boyfriend is so critical sometimes. I remind myself he's an engineer. Recently, he found three cracks on a bridge he inspected. The former two engineers had missed those. I am so proud of him. He drives me crazy, he's so slow and methodical. But, when he does something—he always does it well."

Critical thinkers, analytical personalities, thrive on truth and details. Naturally observant, they are prone to critique and correct others and themselves.

Their daily challenge is to look for the beauty, not the broken. To sip from the chipped cup of life, the half-full part. To enjoy, even knowing it is half-empty—grateful for the privilege to taste.

To focus on the strengths, not illuminate the weaknesses of others, including themselves. To allow Jesus to teach them to find the beauty in the world around them, the people beside them, the life within them.

To let love weave those threads into the pattern of their life.

It is comforting to realize when in a relationship with an analytical person, they are dependable, smart and organized. They are ethical and need our admiration and encouragement.

Their God-given nature is tempered by prayer and God's Spirit. Time will not change their default to perform well. The rightness of what they see needs to be validated. However, they need grace for themselves and from others to keep perspective and balance because life is not perfect, nor the people God loves.

56

2 Processor Types (reference Myers-Briggs & Google)

A newly married man said, "I get so frustrated when we have a disagreement. If Joyce is mad at me, she won't talk about it initially. She says she has to *process*, get her head and heart straight. I learned you shouldn't let the sun go down when you are angry, but sometimes she won't talk about it until the next day. I want to fix the problem or misunderstanding and get it over with."

External processors speak as they think. It is not the final conclusion—they may say things they don't really mean or intend, evoking concern in the listener.

- **The challenge** is to listen to the **external thinker** state random and opposing thoughts and possibly ultimatums and not panic as the pendulum swings. They are processing out loud which may sound irrational and contradictory, until their conclusion, which may not be immediate.

Internal processors think before they speak. Unable and unwilling to respond or *even* give an opinion often without some thought. The listening processor may *think* their partner is distant, uninterested.

- **The challenge** is to let the **internal processor** get the information they need (research) and then even if they don't feel they are ready, to prod them for decisions by gentle questioning, not impatience. Often, they need time to process and a future date to deliver their conclusion.

Our pre-marital counselor spoke to each of us after a discussion turned to a complaining session. "Every relationship has this problem. If we were with someone who did things as we do on our time, we wouldn't need the other person. We look for our counterpart. It brings balance to our lives. One needs to be held back, not jump early, the other to be pushed a bit, not to miss out."

❑ Are you an internal or external processor?

Introvert or Extrovert

Typically introverts like alone time and can feel drained by people. Extroverts seek social gatherings and get energy from people. Introverts are quiet, extroverts are outgoing.

❑ Are you an introvert or extrovert?

❑ How does understanding the different personalities protect us from criticism and contempt?

Love Languages

Meeting needs for Love requires understanding and knowledge.

> *My prayer for you is that you will overflow more and more with love for others and at the same time keep on growing in spiritual knowledge and insight. (Philippians 1: 9 TLB)*

Even though we know love is a decision of the will, we want to *feel loved. It is possible* if others know the primary expression of love that *touches our heart.* Gary Chapman authored *The Five Love Languages,* on the bestseller charts for fifteen years. Why? Counselors discovered initially couples needed to know how to express and re-infuse feelings of love into their relationship—to experience love the way they're wired to *feel* loved.

58

1. **Words of Affirmation** ~ Unsolicited compliments and praise.
2. **Quality Time** ~ Undivided attention, no interruptions. Cell phone face down.
3. **Receiving Gifts** ~ Thoughtful gifts mean you think of them and know what they like.
4. **Acts of Service** ~ Anything to help, chores or responsibilities.
5. **Physical Touch** ~ Hugs, pats on the back, holding hands. Loving gazes.

❑ Which of these would you say is your primary love language?

❑ If you are dating someone, ask them their love language and find a way to express your care for them this week.

THE RAPIDS
The Challenging and Unseen

Relationships deepen or
weaken in strong currents
that require extra energy and effort together to stay afloat. If
successful, the joy of completion and growth will strengthen the
bond of intimacy. It takes energy to move forward when things
are challenging, but you have the opportunity to become a
strong team able to overcome many obstacles.

It's time to switch to a kayak, with the smooth glide of the lake
behind you. Those "Not ready" will *not* be exchanging the
rowboat to continue a potentially rewarding, possibly arduous
journey.

> *Agape love, sacrificial love, requires
> commitment and perseverance.*

- When...you meet **the person** who sticks with you and
  continues to work beside you and work it through, in
  spite of the differences, the past, the poor deliveries and
  unintentional or intentional pain—you are receiving and
  giving agape. When you stand with someone and
  believe the best in them and receive the same grace in
  return—you have a true love.

Together you are navigating raging waters in a kayak with little
experience. You both need to sharpen communication and
response, rowing in sync when sudden logs or boulders appear.
You may feel unsure of your assessment. What is going on with
your partner? Where is God in the white water crisis?

❑ What are some situations a relationship could encounter that create intensity?

❑ What feelings could surface that may need to be addressed?

"My younger son, Jason, recently broke his engagement, after his older brother married last year." Jason's mom smiled. "I knew his fiancé a long time—she was a really sweet girl and we liked her."

"How did he come to that decision?" I prodded.

"Last year Jason travelled to South America for a mission trip. He is very adventurous and loves to climb mountains. However, his fiancé wanted to get married and start having babies.

"One day after his return, Jason came home and said, 'Mom, I thought about what you always told me. When you marry, marry someone you're passionate about. Marry someone you would want to go places with and be with and can't wait to talk to. Someone you think of when you go to bed at night and first thing when you wake up in the morning...I have to break up. I don't have that passion.'"

> *Marry someone you want to be with—not someone you need to be with.*

Even those close to us have failed us—and we have failed them. However, the less we expect someone else to fulfill us and make us happy—the more content we will be. Have you heard, "If you can be content single, you can be content married?"

"I'm glad I married in my thirties," the woman explained. "*I wouldn't have been able to deal with* my husband's anorexia if I married earlier.

"It's like the story of the Velveteen Rabbit... 'Once you are real you can't be ugly except to people who can't understand.'"

61

❑ Share the classic story of the Velveteen Rabbit together (book, audio or video). Discuss how it touches your heart and emotions and why it may have helped this woman.

Integrity means whole, true. Undivided in motive of heart or principle.

> *"...Teacher, we know that you are a man of integrity. You aren't swayed by men because you pay no attention to who they are: but you teach the way of God in accordance with the truth..." (Mark 12:14)*

❑ How are we to be like Jesus? (see Psalm 25:21)

❑ How do you earn and keep trust in a relationship? (see Proverbs 11:3)

Giving Grace

Give grace for the gaps

There will be times when you must offer grace (the gift of forgiveness) to fill your partner's gaps and times they overlook yours, giving grace.

> *He who cannot forgive breaks the bridge over which he himself must pass.*
> ~ George Herbert

❑ How can you apply these verses when unkind words or actions have brought regret?

> *Above all, love each other deeply, because love covers over a multitude of sins. (1 Peter 4:8)*

> *But where sin increased, grace increased all the more. (Romans 5:20)*

❑ In Matthew 18:22, why do you think Jesus answered Peter's question, of how frequently he must forgive his brother, *"I tell you, not seven times, but seventy-seven times?"*

> *Expect change to happen...very, very, very slowly.*

Waiting for Change

A friend realized in her engagement period, "I cannot keep up with Peter's energy level. He can keep going and I just need more sleep and time. I have to continually remind him I cannot do as much as he does in one day."

At the same time she also became frustrated as goals they planned seemed to get shuffled and squashed beneath other things. They married.

One day she wrote, "I have found much more peace as I have laid aside my expectations and realized—I will always be waiting for Peter."

We must decide **what is intentional annoying behavior and what is just inherent behavior** and different from who we are. Attempting to change something inherent is like asking a squirrel to walk the pace of an elephant. It is an impossible.

❑ What do we do if someone's behavior annoys us?

❑ How do we decide what we can ignore and what we can't in a relationship?

> *We must change in ways that help us to move forward better as a team.*
>
> *Change means that we stop using trigger words or act in a manner that intentionally hurts our partner.*

❑ What actions or habits do you have that have been addressed by others? What was your response and what have you changed, or not?

❑ What is something in the person you are dating, you have addressed and has not changed? Is it something you may need to learn to not take personally?

Deep Feelings

Grow as respect grows and needs are met

The #1 need in a relationship is security.

The #2 need is meaningful communication.

"Security comes from communication. How we communicate value to the person we're with makes them feel special."
~ Gary Smalley

Congruence

Do our (or their) words and actions line up?

- If I tell someone it's my birthday and they plan to do something else without me what does that communicate to me? I'm not valued and I *will feel* insecure.

- If I say I love someone and include everyone else but them in my schedule, they *will feel* insecure.

Helpful Questions

- What can I change or do that would make you feel I am listening?

- How can I love you more? What am I not giving you?

My friend spoke from the Valley of Decision as she pondered marriage. "I kept waiting and praying to hear from God. I struggled with the prospect of sharing my finances. I'd been living alone for five years in a house I loved, but would need to leave if we married. We took a vacation with his family and during that time I strongly battled my emotions.

"Some interactions had left me feeling on edge, dismissed and disrespected, but I never had an opportunity to address them in private, our schedule was so hectic. He didn't know. He thought everything was okay. I waited for the right time to talk and when I could finally bring up the anger and pain I'd been carrying, he responded. 'I'm so sorry, I didn't even know. I would never want to hurt you intentionally.' Tears appeared as he explained, 'You are the woman I love and feel we have a future together.'

"We talked it all out and he is much more aware of what I need now. He's been going out of his way to make sure he hears me and I feel cherished. His responses have given me the assurance I needed to get married."

❑ Give an example of avoiding a problem.

❑ Why do dismissive responses feel disrespectful?

Focus on the positive, what is working.

Open up the lines of communication. Bring emotion to the table. Ask God to help you speak the truth gently from your heart and not just your head.

You are trying to connect and care.

- Are we okay?
- If not now, is there a time we could talk? You are so important to me, the sooner the better.
- I'm afraid I may have done something to hurt or offend you? I feel distance between us.

Every time we capsize, I feel crushed. *This is it...we're flailing, drowning. How will we flip around now, Lord?*

Somehow, God pushes deeper and stronger than the whirlpool of resistance trapping us. He breaks through our stubbornness with His humility. He guides us through the rumble and roar, the deep current of hurt, anger and irrational emotion. His gentle voice prods us to worship, to pray, to surrender our selfishness and reach for togetherness...a text, a card, a peace offering toward reconciliation.

We obey our way out, pop back up, sputtering—but breathing again, alive. With deep inhalations, we reaffirm our love to each other and trust in Him. I am always amazed—*How did we go from hopeless and stuck...to free and flowing, Lord?*

After five years of marriage, every time the waters rage and we feel overwhelmed, I am humbled. God keeps us intact, and rolls us back to life, as we look up to Him, together for strength. With His help, we continue rowing stronger and saner, committed to our journey and happy to be together. God remains our Center. He is the One who stabilizes us, despite ourselves...despite the rapids.

Marry someone who lives for God and loves you.

Break Ups

IF the Relationship Capsizes and you're swimming to shore alone—trust God is with you both.

You have each learned from one another. Your faith is stronger for the next boat, the next leap and journey as part of a new team, someday. Opportunity will unfold to love and be loved in a special way by a special someone...as surely as flowers bloom each spring.

> *And we know that in all things God works for the good of those who love him, who have been called according to his purpose. (Romans 8:28)*

> *Unless the Lord builds the house, its builder's labor in vain. (Psalm 127:1)*

❑ How can these verses help you to release and heal from a relationship journey that ended?

Sometimes we row too hard.

Insecurity drives us to work harder when **we need to let go**.

Real confidence comes when we know we are complete in God's eyes. He loves us. Then *we can* accept ourselves and stop looking for approval.

> It takes two people to row, to build synchrony in a relationship. We may not always understand the whys but we must not force what is not there. Keep your confidence in God.

Sometimes we know we just can't continue in a relationship.

"I'm not ready"—a valid reason to end a relationship even without knowing why.

Once I pondered and prayed what to do in a relationship. The pastor even called me to meet with him.

"Why won't you marry so and so." Everyone kept saying we were a 'cute couple.' I felt pressure.

"Why are you breaking up with me?" My bf asked.

"I'm sorry to hurt you. I'm not ready to marry. There's a black hole inside me, and every time we are together it just gets bigger."

- **Some people cannot leave the past and move on.** If every attempt to resolve an issue leads to defensiveness and resentment from past issues then you will not be able to move forward.

- **Different values may appear the longer we are with someone.** These can be detrimental to the direction and foundation of the relationship.

When a relationship is right it brings pleasure and fulfillment...not yearning and pain.

A handsome thirty-year-old young man dated a great gal for a year, then broke-up as values collided.

"She chose to spend time with her friends, rather than come to an important family event I asked her to attend. She continued to be critical of my family."

Now, he is out looking for a mate *trusting God's no's.* "Don't be afraid to be alone," he reflected. "If you are unhappy, it's never too late. Never settle, God has a plan for us all...we just don't know it yet."

> *The Lord God is a sun and a shield. He will give grace and glory. NO good thing will He withhold from those who walk uprightly. (Psalm 84:11)*

❑ How can you apply this verse to soothe a broken heart?

❑ Share a time God said no and later you realized it was a blessing.

❑ If you are afraid to break up you may be in an unhealthy or abusive relationship. What could the signs be?

❑ What resources are available to you for help?

HE LEADS ME BESIDE QUIET WATERS

The Point of Decision

And restores my soul (Psalm 23:2–3)

The trials have either deepened your love and commitment, forging your future destiny with each victory, or one or both of you feel retreat or defeat—and prepare to return to the docking place to regain perspective and composure.

Hopefully, each of you is practicing trust, confident in God's timing and His yes's as well as His no's.

❑ Do you each **add** or bring something positive and irreplaceable to the other person's life?

❑ Read 1 Corinthians 13:4–13. How can you apply this now?

Marriage Myth Busters

Marriage is 50/50

The husband gives up his life for his wife and the wife lays down her life for her husband. There are times you give 100%. Love doesn't record time and effort. Aim for fairness.

I'm counting on No Surprises after marriage

Daily life with a prince or princess dashes the intrigue of courtship. Often we do not really know someone until we marry. We have not seen their triggers and expectations within marriage. Or maybe, *even* hidden habits and hang-ups carrying further consequences from past sins, cultural or family-of-origin issues, recent divorce or ex's. The past may collide with the present...afterwards.

When we're married it will be easier to do what I need to

In every situation there will be something to deal with in ourselves and others—probably not in God's perfect plan. We are either in a trial, coming out of a trial, or going into a trial. We need *to trust that the mate God* has for each of us will accept those things in our past, present and future that have made and continue to make us the people He wants us to be.

I'm not getting married if I see Giants in the land

Each couple *will have giants* to face, some sooner than others. They may even be aware of the giants before marriage— finances, health issues, job challenges, family discord. In the book of Numbers 13–14, twelve spies were sent to scout entry to the Promised Land after wandering years in the desert. Ultimately, only two, Joshua and Caleb, would be allowed to enter. God said they had a different spirit...the spirit of overcoming (Numbers 14:24). The others were fearful. Courage and stepping past fear forge the path of marriage.

We have an enemy

Faith in God's power and perspective from each believer is required in marriage to defeat the enemy who will try to destroy your joyful union by mind battles. The demon of *doubt is often the invisible saboteur* behind accusations and suspicions, real and imagined, spoken or silent...you will encounter that question your mate's love and respect—or your own.

I am equipped to handle Giants

Only God can equip you with the discernment and power to claim your territory, your marriage, and honor your mate. Knowing you sought God's will and He led you into the battles you face with the person who is beside you, will bring peace that passes understanding. Convinced He picked you both as a team to enter the land of promise together, He will slay every plan to defeat you and keep making good things good and the bad things better, as you both walk with Him. *His love never fails.* He will never leave or forsake either of you.

Marriage is overrated

Marriage is as good as you both make it. When are we done remodeling a fixer-upper? If you are unhappy single you will be unhappy married. The storms of life will come, and pass. But expect in marriage to have connection, someone to be present with you in life and to feel emotionally close and bonded. And most of the time, to be headed toward God's wholeness, holiness, despite each of your shortcomings ...together. Be the person now, you would want to marry and after marriage, keep striving to love your mate with a clear conscience before God.

72

Love provides endless opportunities to take one more chance at a time.

She didn't know exactly why she pulled out—but she did. I was there when she found the yellow rose he had left on her porch with a sweet note attached...that God bless her life ahead, without him. He didn't demand answers or berate her for her lack of knowing why she did what she did. And she loved him for it.

She decided to see a counselor and soon realized fear had stopped her. Fear from an alcoholic family history and a failed brief first marriage. She began to seek God's will for them again as she recalled, "I never heard a great big yes, I never had a spiritual experience where I knew God had spoken to me. But, I did realize the love kept growing, 'on and on' as Amy Grant sang. I prayed, 'God, if this is from You, just let it keep going.' It never stopped. Thirty years and two children later, I never heard a no."

Jesus will work His miracles into our everyday world. The miracle of two becoming one. The minds' bendings, the hearts' leadings, and the Lord's concern for our love life in this journey we take to attempt the next stroke. He is faithful. He has been faithful.

He will prove to be **faithful** as we are real with Him and give and receive the love He created us for. The kind of love that renews our life and overcomes...because it is wider, higher and deeper than any chasm that separates us from each other, ourselves, or our Captain.

And now these three remain: faith, hope and love. But the greatest of these is love. (1 Corinthians 13:13)

Bibliography and Recommended Reading

Spiritually Centered
The Purpose Driven Life, Rick Warren
Growing Strong in the Seasons of Life, Chuck Swindoll
Crazy Love, Francis Chan

Self-Aware
The Armor of God, Priscilla Schirer, Lifeway
Spirit Controlled Temperament, Dr. Tim LaHaye.
Please Understand Me II, Dr. David Keirsey (Keirsey.com—overview of 4 temperaments)
Dr. John Trent and Gary Smalley, the Personality Test
Myers-Briggs Personality Assessment, https://www.mbtionline.com/

Self-Control
Eros Defiled, John White
Redeeming Sex, Debra Hirsch
Your Single Treasure, Pastor Rick Stedman
The Invisible Bond, How to Break Free from your Sexual Past, Barbara Wilson

Relationship Smart
Love is a Decision, Gary Smalley
Love and Respect, Dr. Emerson Eggerichs
His Needs Her Needs List, Dr. Willard F. Harley Jr.
Sacred Marriage, Gary Thomas
Marital Intelligence, Gil Steiglitz
Biola Student Resource Center for Marriage and Family Relations

Stable Sensitivity
Five Love Languages, Gary Chapman, www.5lovelanguages.com
Happily Ever After: Finding Grace in the Messes of Marriage, Francis Chan, John Piper, Nancy Leigh-DeMoss
The Seven Principles for Making Marriage Work, Dr. John Gottman
How We Love, Milan and Kay Yerkovich

About the Author

Dee spent the first half of her life single. A hospital nurse, who worked various floors, trauma, ER and recovery units, she also substituted as an elementary school teacher, traveled and loved hiking and the great outdoors.

She has over twenty-five years' experience with Christian Singles ministry, prayer, missions ministries and the Juvenile Justice Chaplaincy (JJC). Dee claims she accompanied, Jasmine, her simple acoustic guitar, in leading worship at the JJC and campfires w single groups. Her newest passion is applying spiritual disciplines to Pilates with yoga.

She met her creative multi-talented husband, Steve, (audio engineer, video editor, musician, chef-like cook) after fulfilling her dream to write a book. *Lord of the Ringless*, *40 devotions and Bible studies*, encourages single believers to live Christ-centered, purposeful lives as they date to meet their someone special while pursuing their dreams. Steve produced and engineered the audiobook nominated for the 2010 Audie-award for the faith-based, non-fiction category.

A dog-lover, *dogSpirations*, *Little Life Lessons, Big God Glimpses*, are animal inspired devotions. Relatable dog stories pet owners experience unveil an understanding of God, ourselves and others. Most were fueled by her endearing yellow Lab named Sam and mini-schnauzers she has loved.

Dee's published poetry, devotions, and animal & human interest stories are found in compilations for Barbour, Revel, Guideposts, CBN and more. She resides with Steve and their dog, Benji, in Northern California. Visit Dee at her blog website DeeAspin.com

www.ingramcontent.com/pod-product-compliance
Lightning Source LLC
Chambersburg PA
CBHW072154020426
42334CB00018B/1998